CW01306790

You Can't BUILD A HOUSE IF YOU'RE A HIPPO

A Book About ALL KINDS OF HOUSES

Fred Ehrlich, M.D.
pictures by Amanda Haley

BLUE APPLE

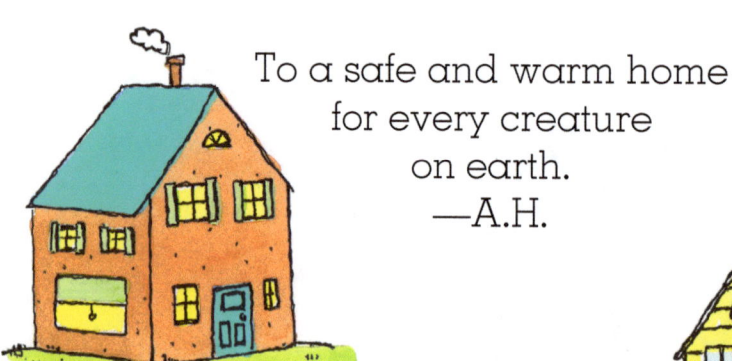

To a safe and warm home
for every creature
on earth.
—A.H.

Text copyright © 2014 by Fred Ehrlich
Illustrations copyright © 2014 by Amanda Haley
All rights reserved
CIP data is available

Published in the United States 2014 by
 Blue Apple Books
South Orange, New Jersey
www.blueapplebooks.com

Contents

INTRODUCTION
Hippo House

CHAPTER ONE
Shells as Homes

CHAPTER TWO
Nests as Homes

CHAPTER THREE
Other Nests

CHAPTER FOUR
Furry Animal Houses

CHAPTER FIVE
Houses for People

Introduction

Hippo House

No hut, or nest, or igloo?
A hippo will not fuss—
A home or shelter is simply not
A hippopota-must!

Hippos don't build houses,
But they surely do OKAY,
Living out their lives
In a hippopota-way!

Hippos live in warm places. They don't need houses, or any kind of shelter, to survive. To keep cool during the heat of the day, they spend a lot of time in water, or wallowing in mud.

Wherever they live, people must have houses. Houses are places to sleep, to eat, to keep clean and safe, and to enjoy family life. Most people would not like to spend all day in the water, or wallowing in mud.

What kind of house do you live in?

From the igloos of the far north to the grass huts around the equator, houses must be built to help people live comfortably and safely in different parts of the world.

EQUATOR

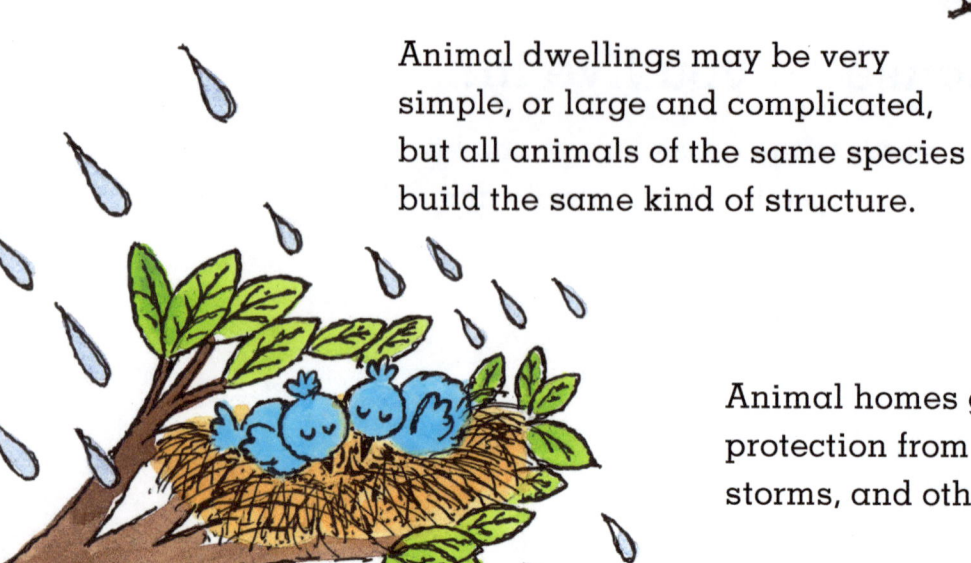

Animal dwellings may be very simple, or large and complicated, but all animals of the same species build the same kind of structure.

Animal homes give protection from cold, heat, storms, and other animals.

They may be used to store food and attract mates and are places to raise babies and create communities.

Some, like a chimpanzee's sleeping nest, may be put together quickly and used for only one night. Others, like termite mounds, may be built over a number of years and last for decades.

What are the only animals that can plan and build houses any way they want them to be? That would be humans—like you and me!

Chapter 1
Shells as Homes

Snails

For some small animals, their houses are part of their bodies. An old saying goes, "snails carry their houses on their backs." This means that a snail's house is its shell.

As the snail's body gets bigger, more shell is added. The snail's body can stick out of the openings in its shell, but it can never come out completely.

A snail moves slowly, slowly,
Leaving a slimy track.
Hey, you'd move slowly, too,
With a house upon your back!

Most snails are small, but not the giant African land snail! It can grow to be one and a half feet long!

Turtles

A turtle's shell is made of about 50 bony plates grown together and covered with a hard top. Its shell grows bigger as it gets larger. The turtle always has "shell-ter."

A turtle can stick its head, legs, and tail out from openings between the top and bottom of its shell. When there is danger, the turtle pulls itself inside its shell to stay safe.

The hinge-back tortoise has added protection—a hinge at the back of its shell. It digs a hole in the dirt, then turns its back to the opening of the hole. When it closes the hinge-flap, other animals cannot attack it from behind.

A hard roof on top,
A sturdy floor below,
A shell home is right
For a turtle on the go.

In lakes, deserts, or forests,
Wherever it crawls or roams,
Its address stays the same—
A turtle's always home.

Crabs and Lobsters

When the bodies of lobsters and crabs start to grow too big for their shells, they crawl out of the old shells and grow new ones. This is called *molting*. Molting is a dangerous time because their bodies are unprotected until a new shell grows and hardens.

The molted shells of crabs wash up on beaches. Did you ever step on one? Ouch!

Horseshoe Crabs

Did you know that horseshoe crabs were on earth before there were dinosaurs—almost 450 million years ago? They are considered to be "living fossils" with a house-shell that hasn't changed much in all that time.

Horseshoe crabs can grow up to 24 inches long. There are no lights or lamps in their shell houses, but horseshoe crabs do have several sets of eyes—and blue blood!

Before the caveman had his cave,
Before the dinosaurs stomped and raved,
Before horseshoes were a sign of luck,
Horseshoe crabs swam in muck!

Each year, upon a certain date,
Horseshoe crabs crawl up the beach
To meet and then to mate.

When eggs are laid, they leave at night,
To return when the time is right.

Chapter 2
Nests as Homes

Have you ever found a bird's nest? Probably yes!
Think all nests are made of sticks and are found in trees?
They're not!

Big and little nests

The brush turkey makes a huge nest out of sticks, leaves, and dirt. It can be 9-12 feet wide and four and a half feet high! No tree could hold such a heavy nest, so they are built on the ground.

A tiny hummingbird nest is one inch across—about the size of a doll's teacup—and might be lined with "borrowed" spiderweb silk.

What's the nest made of?

Birds use whatever is nearby to build their nests. A bird near a beach might use shells. A house finch uses anything it finds—scraps of paper, loose trash, a baby's sock!

The male bowerbird likes to decorate its bower with anything blue, colorful, or shiny that it can find and carry. Hopefully a female bird will find the nest beautiful and be its mate, but the nest is never used to lay eggs or to raise chicks.

How are nests made?

Birds use their own saliva and feathers, and, of course, their beaks and feet to construct nests.

Where to build the nest?

Birds will place their nests in tree branches, in holes in trunks, on cliff ledges, in unused flowerpots, caves, on park statues—all over the place!

The goal is to choose a spot that is big and strong enough for the size of the nest—a place that will give the bird and its eggs and hatchlings protection from weather and other animals.

Swans just put a few sticks around themselves on the ground and—poof!—they're done!

Best Nest

Which nest is best?
Nests in trees? Nests on cliffs?
Nests facing east?
Or those facing west?

Birds know the answers.
Birds from near and far!
The best nest depends upon
The kind of bird you are!

Chapter 3
Other Nests

Bees

Bees' nests are also called hives. They are made of many different materials. Inside the hive are hundreds of little six-sided compartments joined together to form what is called the honeycomb.

Each compartment is made out of wax, which the bees excrete from their bodies. The whole honeycomb is strong, water-resistant and able to hold pollen, bee eggs, and the honey the bees make.

See those busy bodies!
Hear that busy buzz?
Night and day, all work, no play!
That's what a busy bee does!

Beekeepers make wooden bee-houses to help the bees with their work. But bees were making their hives millions of years before there were people on earth.

Wasps

Paper wasps chew up bits of wood to make the paper to build their nests.

STAY AWAY

Paper wasps build with paper,
Potter wasps use clay.
But when you see a wasp nest,
You'd best stay far away!

Potter wasps use bits of clay to make a jar-type nest. They place dead caterpillars inside. When their eggs hatch, the larvae will eat the caterpillars until they can go out and get food for themselves.

Fish

Salmon sweep away sand and gravel with their fins and tails. This makes a shallow nest in which to lay their eggs.

Paradise fish make bubble nests. The male gulps air, then burps it out with little bits of mucus to make bubbles that rise to the surface.

When there are enough bubbles to make a nest, the male and female join together to make fertilized eggs that rise up into the nest.

I'm a paradise fish.
I burp and burp and bubble.
I build bubbly, bubbly nests
So my eggs are safe from trouble!

Chapter 4
Furry Animal Houses

Furry animals live in all kinds of nests.
Some are above the ground; others are deep below.

Dormouse

The tiny dormouse builds a ball-shaped nest of grasses
in a spot where it will be well-hidden in the undergrowth.
The dormouse sleeps in this nest throughout the winter.

Peek-a-boo, dormouse!
Are you asleep in there?
Will you come out of your dor-house
When spring is in the air?

Pygmy Shrew

One of the smallest mammals in the world is the two-inch-long
pygmy shrew. It chooses unused or abandoned burrows
of other animals as its home base.

A pygmy shrew must consume one and a half times
its weight every day. This means it has to catch and
eat something every 15-20 minutes, day and night.
No wonder it doesn't have time to build its own burrow!

Woodchuck

Take a look at a woodchuck's face and you'll see that its eyes, ears, and nose are located near the top of its head. This makes it easier for the woodchuck to peer over the rim of its two-foot-long burrow in order to know if there's anything dangerous nearby.

How can you tell if a burrow belongs to a woodchuck?
If there's a big mound of dirt near the main entrance, it probably does!

Moles

Moles are built for burrowing! Long snouts that can push dirt aside and front paws like little shovels make them great at digging tunnels. A mole is not very fast or strong and has poor eyesight. Luckily, its mighty network of tunnels makes it hard to catch!

> To dig its home-y burrow out,
> A mole uses claws and snout.
> A woodchuck makes a mighty mound,
> Removing dirt from underground.
> In the burrow-battle of 'chuck and mole—
> Who will dig the grandest hole?

Badgers

Badgers are good housekeepers. They keep their burrows clean and have a separate outdoor place for their toilet activities.

Housecleaning

I sweep my burrow floor.
I clean out all debris.
It may be just a hole,
But this is home to me!

Badgers dig large underground dens with many tunnels connecting separate rooms, or chambers. Often, several families of badgers will share the same den. Badgers like company!

Welcome

Sleepover

Come on down,
Bring a friend,
Or two, or six, or ten!
There's always room
To spare and share
In every badger den.

Wolves

Wolf dens are only used for birthing baby wolves—which are called pups or puppies.

A hollow log, or a space between big rocks, is a place that wolves might choose for their den. If it's a really good den, it will be used over and over again by many different wolf mothers.

I am not the first to use
This deep and sturdy crack,
But this will be a perfect den
To raise a wolf-ie pack!

Foxes

A fox will often take over some part of a large badger den. This saves the fox from having to dig its own holes. But badgers don't like the smell of the foxes and block up the passages between the parts of the burrow the fox has taken over.

P.U.! The foxes are moving in!

Beavers

Beavers are great builders. Their dexterous paws, wide flat tails, and big sharp teeth make great tools! Many beavers work together to create their stick-and-mud homes, called lodges.

Before they build a lodge, the beavers create a pond by loading up a waterway with piles of sticks and logs, called dams.

Lodges are built on top of the water in the pond. They usually have two rooms and can only be entered by swimming in from underneath. One room is used for drying off; one is used for daily living and raising kits.

When a lodge needs repair, beavers are on the job! Their homes must last through winter and storms.

A beaver gives a mighty slap
With its tail so flat and wide.
The noise alerts the beaver kits,
"It's time to duck and hide."

Prairie Dogs

Prairie dogs live in large colonies called towns.
There may be a thousand in one town.
With all the yips and chirps going on,
they can be quite noisy!

They build complicated underground burrows
with many chambers and tunnels.
You'll see little prairie pup heads popping
out of the many exit holes!

Some of the older prairie dogs will stand guard—
looking for eagles or other predators.
Younger prairie dogs love to play with one another.
They tumble and roll down hills together.
If a guard dog sees danger, it makes a warning sound.

All of the prairie dogs dive into their tunnels for safety.

Listen Up!
Prairie dogs are not dogs,
But they do bark and nip.
When danger comes around their town,
They yelp, "Yip-yip-yip!"

Chimpanzee

Each night, chimpanzees build a new rough nest for sleeping. Choosing strong places high up in trees, it takes them just three to five minutes to bend branches together to make a comfortable place to sleep.

Pick a spot,
Bend some branches
For a minute or three.
Soon you'll rest in your nest,
If you're a chimpanzee!

Chapter 5
Houses for People

There are more names for the houses people live in than we can fit on this page.

Hut, cabin, igloo, teepee, lodge, yurt, castle, palace, ranch, apartment, cottage, houseboat—the list goes on!

In building their own places to live, humans have learned from, and copied, some of the amazing creations built by animals.

Just like animals, people use:

wood

stone

mud

grasses

dirt

clay

and sand

to build their homes.

But people need something else to help them build—
something that animals do not have.

Could you build a house using just your mouth, hands, feet—
and maybe a little spit? I don't think so!
Humans had to invent tools to make hand-built houses
like cabins, teepees, igloos, and huts.

Don't have long, sharp teeth
like a beaver?
You need an axe
or a handsaw.

Can't produce enough gooey saliva to
hold things together?
Try using a hammer, nails,
screwdriver, and screws.

What does EVERY home need to have?
Take a look at this house. How does it compare to your house?

What do some homes have that others don't?

Heat
This might come from a fireplace, stove, or heating system. If your house was in the desert, do you think it would need to be heated?

Air-conditioning
On hot, sticky days, air-conditioning makes a house more comfortable. Do you think homes near the North Pole have air-conditioning?

Running Water and Electricity

Most houses in the US have these things to help us shower, use a toilet and sink, and provide power for refrigerators, lights, televisions, computers, etc.

In parts of the world that don't have pipes that provide water for houses, people get water from lakes, streams, or rivers. Or, they might dig wells to reach water that lies deep in the ground. To be safe to drink or use, this water has to be boiled or treated with chemicals. It's much easier to turn on a faucet!

Housing Needs

Here's a house with a good roof.
This makes it very waterproof!

Let in light! Banish gloom!
Windows brighten up a room.

A room to eat or sleep or pee?
Walls give us privacy!

Like lights, computers, and TV?
Hooray for electricity!

My home has four strong walls,
A solid roof, and floor.

I can't stay inside all day.
That's why I built a door!

Moving: More Space? A New Place?

Because your skin grows as you get bigger and taller, you'll never molt like a crab—no matter how big you get! But when families get bigger, they may move to a house with more space. When kids grow up and move away, parents may decide to live in a smaller home.

People can change the way that they house themselves in ways that animals cannot.

Animals can only make very slight differences to adapt to a place or new condition. Birds do this by choosing some unusual places to build a nest.

*Is a tree always a nesting spot?
Mostly, yes. But sometimes...not!
You never know what a bird might choose.
A traffic light? Un-used shoes?
If it's a quiet or out-of-reach spot,
A bird might think, "Well, why not?"
No one's using a mailbox?
A bird won't need a key.
She'll just open the door and chirp...
Welcome home to me!*

What kinds of houses would you like to try living in?
Would you bundle up for a week in an igloo?
Lose your shoes and spend a month in a grass hut?

Best Builders

Who are the best home-builders—people or animals?

No human, no matter how skilled and patient, can make a perfect honeycomb like the honeybee, or a woven nest like the weaver bird.

But we are the only animal who can build many different kinds of houses and invent new ways to build.

And a hippo? It's not a house builder and doesn't need to be. It protects its skin by living in water and mud. It cannot carry any food, so it needs to live close to what it can eat. It cannot survive where it's cold, so warm places are the only place you'll find hippos.

Even without a house, hippos are right where they need to be. Hooray for the hippo!

Be grateful for the home you have.
It's right where you need to be, too!

Small and neat, with just enough?

Large and roomy, filled with stuff?

Quiet and private?

An amazing view?

Full of lively buzz and hum?

What says "home" to you?

my home

CPSIA information can be obtained
at www.ICGtesting.com
Printed in the USA
LVHW021515281021
701819LV00002B/85